EQUITY AND FAIRNESS

ANNA BERRIGAN

PowerKiDS press™

Published in 2023 by The Rosen Publishing Group, Inc.
2544 Clinton Street, Buffalo, NY 14224

First Edition

Editor: Greg Roza
Book Design: Michael Flynn

Photo Credits: Cover wavebreakmedia/Shutterstock.com; (series background) tavizta/Shutterstock.com; pp. 5, 14, 15 Krakenimages.com/Shutterstock.com; p. 6 Rawpixel.com/Shutterstock.com; p. 7 SeventyFour/Shutterstock.com; p. 9 Sthanlee B. Mirador/Sipa USA/AP Images; p. 10 lev radin/Shutterstock.com; p. 11 Veja/Shutterstock.com; p. 13 Konrad Kmiec/Shutterstock.com; p. 17 Prostock-studio/Shutterstock.com; p. 19 Pierre Teyssot/Shutterstock.com; p. 21 https://commons.wikimedia.org/wiki/File:Red_Cloud_by_John_K_Hillers_circa_1880.jpg; p. 22 Lee Snider Photo Images/Shutterstock.com; p. 23 Everett Collection/Shutterstock.com; p. 25 miker/Shutterstock.com; p. 26 David Smart/Shutterstock.com; p. 27 Antwon McMullen/Shutterstock.com; p. 29 https://commons.wikimedia.org/wiki/File:Photograph_of_White_House_Meeting_with_Civil_Rights_Leaders._June_22,_1963_-_NARA_-_194190_(no_border).tif.

Library of Congress Cataloging-in-Publication Data

Names: Berrigan, Anna, author.
Title: Equity and Fairness / Anna Berrigan.
Description: Buffalo, New York : PowerKids Press, [2023] | Series: Spotlight on a
   fair and equal society | Includes index.
Identifiers: LCCN 2021058156 (print) | LCCN 2021058157 (ebook) | ISBN
   9781538388082 (library binding) | ISBN 9781538388051 (paperback) | ISBN
9781538388099 (ebook)
Subjects: LCSH: United States--Race relations--Juvenile literature. |
   African Americans--History--Juvenile literature. | Indians of North
   America--History--Juvenile literature. | Racism--United States--Juvenile
   literature. | Equality--United States--Juvenile literature.
Classification: LCC E184.A1 K488 2023 (print) | LCC E184.A1 (ebook) | DDC
   305.800973--dc23/eng/20211214
LC record available at https://lccn.loc.gov/2021058156
LC ebook record available at https://lccn.loc.gov/2021058157

Manufactured in the United States of America

Some of the images in this book illustrate individuals who are models. The depictions do not imply actual situations or events.

CPSIA Compliance Information: Batch #CSPK23. For further information contact Rosen Publishing at 1-800-237-9932.

Find us on

CONTENTS

CHAPTER ONE

WHAT IS EQUITY?

Equity means making sure that everyone has what they need to thrive. Doing what is fair may not mean that everyone gets the same exact thing. Fairness may mean treating people differently so that their needs are met. This is how justice works. Equity depends on **empathy** and caring about other people's needs.

What if everyone in your class is given the same amount of time for a test? Would this same time limit be unfair for the needs of a classmate who is learning to speak and read English? More time for that student would be fair. Students using remote learning during the COVID-19 **pandemic** needed equity of access to Wi-Fi, tablets, and even desks. Some did not have what they needed. Equity closes gaps so that human needs are met.

Fairness is the need to solve a problem like being able to see a baseball game on a crowded playground. How could younger, shorter kids and older, taller kids all get to see the game?

CHAPTER TWO

FAIRNESS CLOSE TO HOME

Understanding equity can be the first step toward a fair and equal society. Empathy, fair decisions, and action for change can turn injustice into justice. Inequality and unfairness in your community, school, or neighborhood are part of a much bigger picture across America and across centuries.

Having shoes to wear is a basic need for every kid. Equity means meeting that need. As a five year old, Nicholas Lowenger visited a homeless shelter with his mom and felt sad to see so many kids wearing torn-up shoes. Working in Nicholas' garage, he and his peers collected new shoes for 45,000 kids in 36 states.

Paying attention to equity and inequity in your world builds awareness and understanding that could lead to change. You might even be part of making change happen. Many young people have succeeded in creating equitable solutions for problems. Using her voice, Mina Fedor, 13, organized a 2021 rally to stop violence against Asian Americans, and 1,200 people from her town in California participated. Khloe Joiner, 9, has shared 18,000 donated books with Texas kids and hopes to share a million.

CHAPTER THREE

POSITIVE AND DETERMINED

When Orion Jean was only five years old, he won $500 in a kids kindness contest. He **donated** it to a children's hospital in his town in Texas. Kindness became his goal in life. Orion and his **allies** organized Thanksgiving food donations in 2020 that supplied 100,000 meals to people without enough to eat. Orion also worked to solve the problem of book **scarcity** by making 50,000 books available to kids who needed them.

On March 7, 2022, Orion Jean was selected as *Time* Magazine's Kid of the Year for his contributions to making the world a better place. Orion's boundless actions to meet the needs of others started with seeing something that made him sad. Empathy put Orion into motion to solve problems. He encourages people to see unfairness in society and to step up to fix it.

At 11 years old, Orion Jean sees the world through caring eyes and takes action for change. Orion is a leader and an inspiration to people all over the world.

CHAPTER FOUR

ROLE MODELS FOR EQUITY AND ACTION

Countless athletes, musicians, celebrities, and people in your own community have used their time and **resources** to build a more fair and equitable society. Joe Burrow is known for winning the Heisman Trophy, the biggest honor in college football, and leading the Cincinnati Bengals to the Super Bowl. As he reached these **achievements** in football, he had another goal in mind.

JOE BURROW

When those who have resources take action to help others, the gap between those with plenty and those with not enough closes.

Many people in his hometown—Athens, Ohio—faced poverty and hunger. Burrow used his Heisman speech to raise awareness of hunger suffered by the families in his town. His empathy for kids who go home hungry after school raised a strong response. Donations and funds poured in to the Athens County Food Pantry and continue to do so. By caring about inequity, Joe Burrow showed he was more than just a great quarterback.

CHAPTER FIVE

WHEN THE WORLD RESPONDS

In 2022, millions of Ukraine's people, including many children, escaped the bombs, fires, and guns of war by fleeing their country. These people often needed everything when they got to safety. This earned the empathy of most of the world. News media shared photos of children holding stuffed animals and bundled in winter coats and hats. They were part of millions who crossed into nearby countries to survive.

How do millions of people find food, shelter, medical care, and safety? Countries such as Poland welcomed them with water, food, blankets, diapers, and medicine. Leaders and **volunteers** turned any open spaces in buildings into shelters. People opened their homes and schools and shared every kind of support. Organizations such as Doctors Without Borders, World Central Kitchen, UNICEF, CARE, and the United Nations rushed to provide what was needed.

People around the world sometimes work together to help refugees.

CHAPTER SIX

WHEN FAIRNESS IS THE SOLUTION

The purpose of equity and fairness is to close the gap between those who have enough and those who don't have enough. That can apply to education, housing, food, clean air and water, health care, and employment.

Young people are able to work with others for fairness and equity far beyond their classrooms.

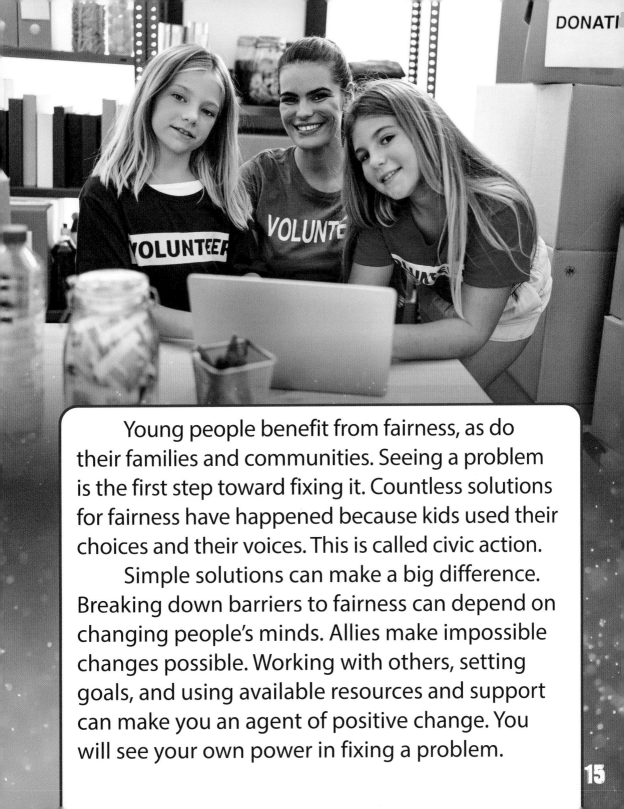

Young people benefit from fairness, as do their families and communities. Seeing a problem is the first step toward fixing it. Countless solutions for fairness have happened because kids used their choices and their voices. This is called civic action.

Simple solutions can make a big difference. Breaking down barriers to fairness can depend on changing people's minds. Allies make impossible changes possible. Working with others, setting goals, and using available resources and support can make you an agent of positive change. You will see your own power in fixing a problem.

CHAPTER SEVEN

CLOSING EQUITY GAPS IN SCHOOLS

Gaps in the quality of school programs are unfair to learners. Safety, school success, caring environments, technology, and opportunities for growth are basic needs. Failing to meet these needs puts students, each with unique needs, at risk. State and community action makes a difference every day. Programs for school lunch and breakfast, support for English language learners, cultural awareness, **mentor** programs, and response to special needs have helped improve equity.

Government data shows that poverty has a strong connection to schools that have shortfalls in helping students. Schools in poorer communities often serve many Black or Hispanic students. Some states have many schools that fall short. Some states and regions have much better success. Educators are working to learn what all learners need. Solutions for these problems can lead to more equity and fairness.

The COVID-19 pandemic slowed progress in closing gaps in equity. Shortages included Internet access, digital tools, teachers, workspaces in homes, social connections, and motivation.

CHAPTER EIGHT

CLOSING EQUITY GAPS IN SPORTS

Female soccer stars, including Olympic champions, earn much less than male soccer stars. Their efforts to get fair pay took years but finally started resulting in a positive change. Women have just begun to work as referees for the National Football League. And in the NFL, as well as at some high schools and colleges, women are starting to take more part in the game. Some women in football are excellent kickers, and kickers win about one of every three football games.

A federal law called Title IX (nine) was passed in 1972 to force colleges and high schools to fund women's teams for competition. The national basketball championships feature men's teams and women's teams in the spotlight. Swimming, diving, tennis, volleyball, running, and many more sports now give more talented athletes opportunities.

Closing equity gaps celebrates talent, skill, and achievement as well as fairness.

CHAPTER NINE

LOOKING BACK: WHO DECIDES WHAT'S FAIR

In the present as well as the past, society has created barriers to equity for many people. Some rules, laws, and ideas ignore the needs of groups and individuals. **Immigrants** seeking safety, work, and basic needs have often faced a desperate struggle for acceptance and fair treatment.

For hundreds of years, the labor of enslaved people made it possible for wealthy landowners to grow crops and make a lot of money in many states. For hundreds of years, without empathy or justice for millions, enslavers denied enslaved people basic human rights and needs. Unwilling to share the land with the native people of the Americas, governments and armies took it, often by force. Because of this, millions of Native Americans lost their homes, identities, lives, and rights. The U.S. Constitution calls for a **census** every 10 years. At first, African Americans and Native Americans weren't counted as citizens.

Consider the words of Red Cloud, an Oglala Lakota leader: "They made us many promises, more than I can remember, but they never kept but one; they promised to take our land, and they took it."

CHAPTER TEN

PAST AND PRESENT: DIGNITY AND RESPECT

In 1750, a rich man named Adolph Philipse died, and people made a list of all his property. The list included 23 people listed as "Negros," often without names. They were considered property to be sold or traded. Today, those who tell the stories of these people at Philipsburg Manor in Tarrytown, New York, talk about "enslaved people" or "enslaved Africans." The words we try to use today reflect the fact that enslaved Africans were human beings, not objects.

PHILIPSBURG MANOR

Some people make fun of immigrants for dressing or speaking differently. Some say they should just blend in. But America has many different kinds of people. Immigration officials used to change the names of U.S. immigrants to something easier (they thought) to say.

Even after slavery ended in the United States, it was still legal to treat African Americans unfairly. It was common and accepted to use unkind words to talk about many people who belonged to different ethnic groups, religions, and cultures. Even when it was accepted behavior, it was never right. All people deserve to be treated with **dignity** and respect, and that begins with the words we use.

CHAPTER ELEVEN

LOOKING BACK: CULTURAL CLASH

When Europeans first arrived in the Americas, there were already many Native American civilizations there. They had their own languages, beliefs, and laws. Native societies tend to focus more on the well-being of the group instead of individual gain. They also tended to be more mindful of the natural world and often took only what they needed to live.

Because this way of life was so different from what European **colonizers** were used to, they viewed Native Americans as uncivilized. Colonial governments, and later the U.S. government, made treaties, or formal agreements, about where Native Americans could live. The government often broke these treaties if the land was good for farming or contained valuable natural resources. Human history repeats this pattern of unfairness and injustice by colonizers, denying human rights and human needs for land, resources, and power.

Many sports teams adopt Native American figures with feather headdresses as mascots. This can be disrespectful to the human dignity and values of Native Americans.

CHAPTER TWELVE

HISTORIC ACTION FOR EQUITY

Abolitionists were people who spoke, wrote, and took action to end slavery. Sojourner Truth, Harriet Beecher Stowe, Frederick Douglass, Harriet Tubman, William Lloyd Garrison, Lucretia Mott, David Walker, and many others took action and made change. Constitutional amendments ended slavery in America after the Civil War.

EMANCIPATION PROCLAMATION

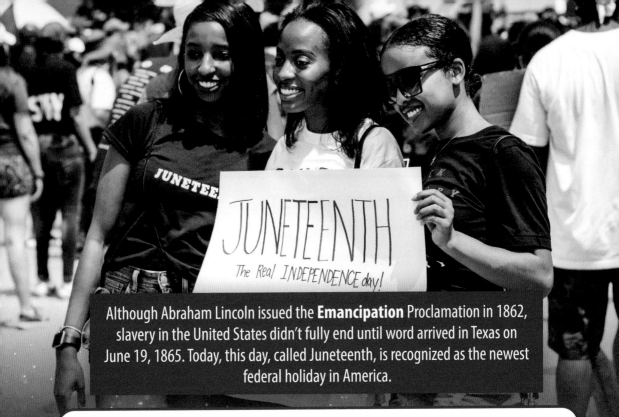

JUNEETEE...

JUNETEENTH
The Real INDEPENDENCE day!

Although Abraham Lincoln issued the **Emancipation** Proclamation in 1862, slavery in the United States didn't fully end until word arrived in Texas on June 19, 1865. Today, this day, called Juneteenth, is recognized as the newest federal holiday in America.

Men, women, and children marched in the streets, waved banners and signs, gave speeches, wrote for newspapers, and worked with political and business leaders for safe and fair conditions for workers, the end of child labor, and better living conditions for the poor. Others worked for a safe food supply, education for children, fairness for immigrants, and civil rights. Strong efforts were needed to win the right to vote for women and Black people. Today, these efforts make our country a better and more equitable place.

CHAPTER THIRTEEN

SEPARATE IS NOT EQUAL

Correcting the injustices of the past can be a hard process. People have different ideas about what is fair and how to make things better. After the Civil War and the end of slavery, some people still treated African Americans unfairly. Some states passed laws that forced African Americans to use side or back entrances to public places or ride in back seats on buses or trains. Generally, there were fewer places African Americans were allowed to go, and those places weren't as nice as places for white people.

In 1955, the U.S. Supreme Court ruled in *Brown v. Board of Education of Topeka* that **segregation** of schools was illegal. However, many schools in southern states resisted **integration**. In some places, the federal government had to send soldiers to escort African American students to school.

Many organizations and leaders such as Martin Luther King Jr. and John Lewis succeeded in making progress toward equity. Voting rights, education, and fair treatment under the law contribute to equity.

CHAPTER FOURTEEN

WHAT CAN YOU DO?

Changing the way society thinks is a big job, but it begins with you. When you're fair and kind in the things you do and say, you're a positive force for good. Build connections between your feelings, your values, and your actions. Empathize with those who don't have what they need to thrive. Recognize that knowing more about people's lives and experiences helps you grow in awareness. Look at bias and prejudice with honesty. Open your eyes to the possibilities of making this a better world because you see problems and work to solve them.

If you think young people can't help make equitable changes in the world, just read about Greta Thunberg or Malala Yousafzai. They may inspire you! Be sure to register to vote as soon as you're old enough. That's the best way to make sure your voice is heard.

GLOSSARY

achievement (uh-CHEEV-muhnt) A result gained by effort.

ally (AA-ly) A person, group, or nation associated or united with another in a common purpose.

census (SEN-suhs) A counting of the population done by the government.

colonizer (KAH-luh-ny-zuhr) A nation or state that establishes a colony, or an area controlled by another country that's usually far from it. Also, a person who's part of establishing a colony.

dignity (DIG-nuh-tee) The quality of being worthy of honor or respect.

donate (DOH-nayt) To give as a way of helping people in need.

emancipation (ih-man-suh-PAY-shun) The act of setting someone free from control or slavery.

empathy (EHM-puh-thee) The understanding and sharing of the emotions and experiences of another person.

immigrant (IH-muh-grunt) A person who comes to a country to live there.

integration (in-tuh-GRAY-shuhn) The state of bringing different races, genders, or social classes together to form one group.

mentor (MEHN-tohr) Someone who teaches, gives guidance, or gives advice to someone else, especially a less experienced person.

pandemic (pan-DEH-mihk) An outbreak of a disease that occurs over a wide geographic area and typically affects a significant proportion of the population

resource (REE-sors) Something that can be used.

scarcity (SCAYR-suh-tee) Having only a small supply of something, usually not enough for everyone who needs that supply.

segregation (seh-gruh-GAY-shun) The separation of people based on race, class, sex, gender, or ethnicity.

volunteer (vahl-uhn-TEER) Someone who does something to help because they want to do it.

PRIMARY SOURCE LIST

p. 19
Red Cloud. Photo. Taken about 1880 in Washington, D.C. John K. Hillers. Beinecke Rare Book and Manuscript Library, Yale University, New Haven, Connecticut.

p. 22
Philipse family manor house. Photo. Taken in 2009 in Sleepy Hollow, New York. Lee Snider Photo Images. Held by Shutterstock.com.

p. 26
Emancipation Proclamation. Document. 1863. National Archives, Washington, D.C.